An *Unexpected*
Christmas
Guest

As Told by
Alda Ellis

Harvest House Publishers
Eugene, Oregon

andle, candle burning bright

Through our window pane tonight

Like the shining Christmas star

Guiding shepherds from afar

Lead a weary Christmas guest

That he may share our Christmas blessed.

−Alda Ellis

AN UNEXPECTED CHRISTMAS GUEST

Text Copyright ©2001 by Alda Ellis
Published by Harvest House Publishers
Eugene, OR 97402

Library of Congress Cataloging-in-Publication Data
Markham, Edwin, 1852-1940.
    An unexpected Christmas guest / as told by Alda Ellis.
        p. cm.
    Poem originally written by Edwin Markham.
    ISBN 0-7369-0572-3
    1. Christmas—Poetry. I. Ellis, Alda, 1952- II. Title.

PS2362 .U54 2001
811'.52–dc21

Artwork which appears in this book is from the personal collection of
Alda Ellis.

Scripture quotations are from: the HOLY BIBLE: NEW INTERNATIONAL
VERSION ®. NIV ®. Copyright © 1973, 1978, 1984 by the International
Bible Society. Used by permission of Zondervan Publishing House; and
the King James Version of the Bible.

Design and Production by Koechel Peterson & Associates,
Minneapolis, Minnesota.

Printed in China.

01 02 03 04 05 06 07 08 09 10 / IM / 10 9 8 7 6 5 4 3 2 1

When woodsmoke perfumes the winter air and we begin to prepare for the holidays, my family looks forward to sharing a very special story together here in our home at Red Oak Hill. This simple yet cherished holiday tradition—the reading of Edwin Markham's wonderful tale about Conrad the shoe cobbler—always inspires me to embrace the Christmas season. As timely today as when it was first written in 1899, *An Unexpected Christmas Guest* is a celebration of joy and generosity with a delightful glimpse into a Christmas past.

As your Christmas unfolds, it is my hope that you will include this treasured poem as one of your own holiday classics and also share it with friends and loved ones. Conrad's endearing spirit of giving serves as a gentle reminder to all who are wearied by the hurried bustle of the season.

May you and those you love enjoy this version of *An Unexpected Christmas Guest,* for the best gift ever will not be found in a box.

Let us not love in word, neither in tongue; but in deed.

—1 John 3:18

$\mathcal{I}$t happened one day, near
December's white end.
Two neighbors called on
their old-time friend.
And they found his shop,
so meager and mean,
Made gay with a hundred
boughs of green.

$\mathcal{C}$onrad, the cobbler, was stitching
with face a shine,
When he suddenly stopped
as he twitched a twine.

"Old friends, good news! At dawn today,
When the cock was scaring the night away,
The Lord appeared in a dream to me,
And said, 'I am coming your Guest to be.'

"So I've been busy with feet astir,
Strewing the floor with branches of fir.
The table is ready and the kettle is shined,
And over the rafter the holly twined.

"He comes today,
and the table is spread
With milk and honey
and wheatened bread."

So his friends went home;
and his face grew still
As he watched for the shadow
across the sill.
He lived all the moments o'er and o'er
When the Lord should enter
the lowly door—

The knock, the call, the latch pulled up,
The lighted face, the offered cup.

He would wash the feet
where the spikes had been,
He would kiss the hands
where the nails went in,

And then at last would sit with Him
And break the bread as the day grew dim.

While the cobbler mused,
there passed his pane
A beggar drenched by the driving rain—
A shabby beggar, whose shoes were torn
And all of his clothes were ragged and worn.

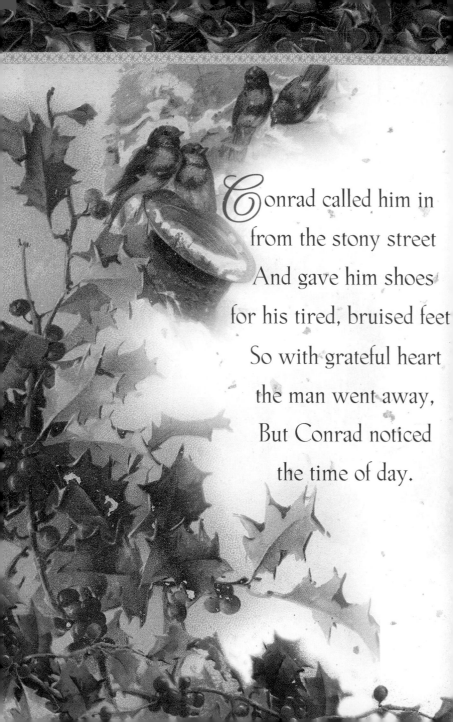

Conrad called him in
from the stony street
And gave him shoes
for his tired, bruised feet
So with grateful heart
the man went away,
But Conrad noticed
the time of day.

He wondered what
made the Lord so late
Or how much longer
would he have to wait.

When he heard a knock,
he ran to the door,
But it was only a stranger
once more—
A bent old lady
with a shawl of black,
A bundle of kindling
piled high on her back.
Her face, with wrinkles
of sorrow sown,
Gave insight to sadness
and hard work she'd known.

Needed for this weary
crone was a rest,
But that was reserved
for Conrad's great Guest.
Conrad brewed her
a fresh steaming cup,
Gave rest for her back
then helped lift it up.

He gave her his loaf
and steadied her load
As she took to her way
on the long weary road.

$\mathcal{T}$hen to his door came a little child,

Lost and afraid in the world so wild.

"Please, help me, and tell me where am I!"

Came out of the still, dark night her cry.

There stood a child
who had wandered away,
Lost from her family
on this Christmas Day.
He called her in
and wiped her tears.
He quieted
all her childish fears.

In the big, dark world, he picked her up
And gave her milk in the waiting cup.
He led her to her mother's arms,
Out of the reach of the world's alarms.

Leading her to
her home once more,
He returned to his own
still darkened door—
And stood disappointed
as twice before.

 he day went down
in the crimson west
And with it the hope
of the blessed Guest.
And Conrad sighed
as the world turned gray,

"Why is it, Lord,
that Your feet delay?
Did You forget
that this was the day?"

*T*hen soft in the silence a Voice he heard:
"Lift up your heart, for I kept My word.
Three times I came to your friendly door;
Three times My shadow
was on your floor.

For I was the beggar with bruised cold feet.

I was the woman you gave something to eat;

And I was the child on the homeless street.

"Three times I knocked,
three times I came in
And each time I found
the warmth of a friend.

"Of all the gifts,
love is the best.
I was honored to be
your Christmas Guest."

For I was hungry and you gave me something to eat,

I was thirsty and you gave me something to drink,

I was a stranger and you invited me in,

I needed clothes and you clothed me...

Whatever you did for one of the least of these brothers of mine,

you did for me.

—MATTHEW 25:35-40